PIANO | VOCAL

Hillsong MODERN WORSHIP HITS

ISBN 978-1-4950-5478-5

HAL•LEONARD®
CORPORATION
7777 W. BLUEMOUND RD. P.O. BOX 13819 MILWAUKEE, WI 53213

In Australia Contact:
Hal Leonard Australia Pty. Ltd.
4 Lentara Court
Cheltenham, Victoria, 3192 Australia
Email: ausadmin@halleonard.com.au

Visit Hal Leonard Online at
www.halleonard.com

ALIVE

Words and Music by AODHAN KING
and ALEXANDER PAPPAS

Lyrics:

I was

lost with a bro-ken heart.
midst of the dark-est night,

You picked me
let Your

up; now I'm set a-part. ___
love be the shin-ing light, ___

From the ash I am born a-gain,
break-ing chains that were hold-ing me.

To Coda

ANCHOR

Words and Music by BEN FIELDING
and DEAN USSHER

I have this

hope

love,

as an an-chor for my ___ soul:

all my fear is swept a - way.

CHRIST IS ENOUGH

Words and Music by REUBEN MORGAN
and JONAS MYRIN

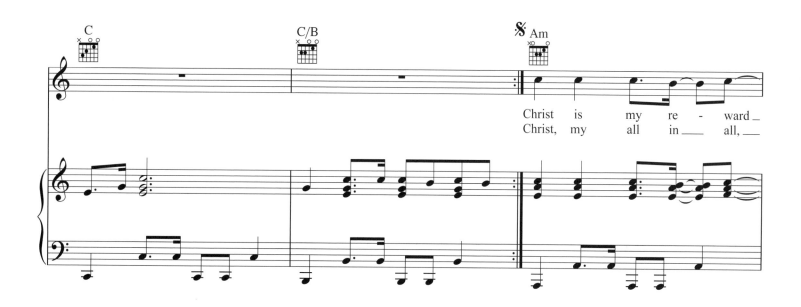

Christ is my re - ward _____
Christ, my all in _____ all, _____

_____ and all of my _ de - vo - tion.
_____ the joy of my _ sal - va - tion.

Now there's
And this

* *Recorded a half step lower.*

BROKEN VESSELS
(Amazing Grace)

Words and Music by JOEL HOUSTON
and JONAS MYRIN

CORNERSTONE

Words and Music by JONAS MYRIN,
REUBEN MORGAN, ERIC LILJERO
and EDWARD MOTE

GOD IS ABLE

Words and Music by REUBEN MORGAN
and BEN FIELDING

Recorded a half step lower.

FOREVER REIGN

Words and Music by REUBEN MORGAN
and JASON INGRAM

HOSANNA

Words and Music by
BROOKE LIGERTWOOD

I see the King of ___ Glo — ry
I see a gen - er - a - tion

com - ing on the clouds with fire. ____ The whole earth ___ shakes, ___
ris - ing up to take their place ____ with self - less faith, ___

Heal my heart and make it clean, __
Break my heart for what breaks Yours, __

o - pen up my eyes to the things un - seen. __
ev -'ry-thing I am for Your king-dom's cause, __

Show me how to love like __ You __ have loved me.
as I walk from earth in - to __

I SURRENDER

Words and Music by
MATT CROCKER

Slowly, in 2

Here I am, down on my knees a-gain, sur-ren-der-ing all, sur-ren-der-ing _____ all. And find me here, Lord, as You draw me

MIGHTY TO SAVE

Words and Music by BEN FIELDING
and REUBEN MORGAN

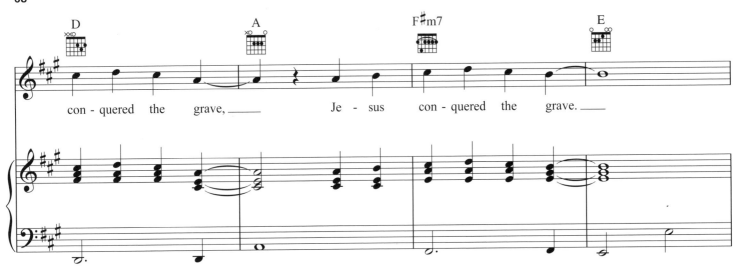

con - quered the grave, _____ Je - sus con - quered the grave. _____

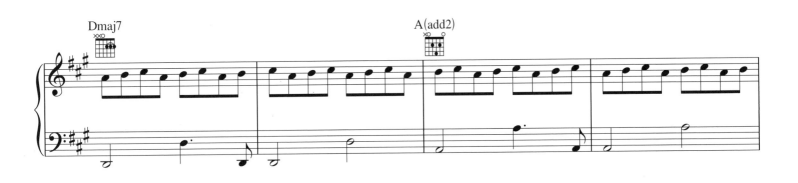

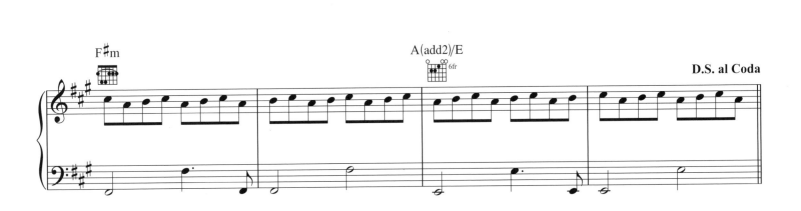

D.S. al Coda

Sav - ior, He can move the

LEAD ME TO THE CROSS

Words and Music by
BROOKE LIGERTWOOD

* *Recorded a half step lower.*

MAN OF SORROWS

Words and Music by BROOKE LIGERTWOOD
and MATT CROCKER

Moderately slow

Man of sor-rows, Lamb of God,
Si-lent as He stood ac-cused,

by His own be-trayed. The sin of man and
beat-en, mocked and scorned. Bow-ing to the

wrath of God has been on Je - sus
Fa-ther's will, He took a crown of

SINKING DEEP

Words and Music by JOEL DAVIES
and AODHAN KING

Stand-ing here in Your pres-ence, in a grace so re-lent-less,
When I'm lost, You pur-sue me, lift my head to see Your glo-ry,

I am won by per-fect love.
Lord of all, so beau-ti-ful.

OCEANS
(Where Feet May Fail)

Words and Music by JOEL HOUSTON,
MATT CROCKER and SALOMON LIGHTHELM

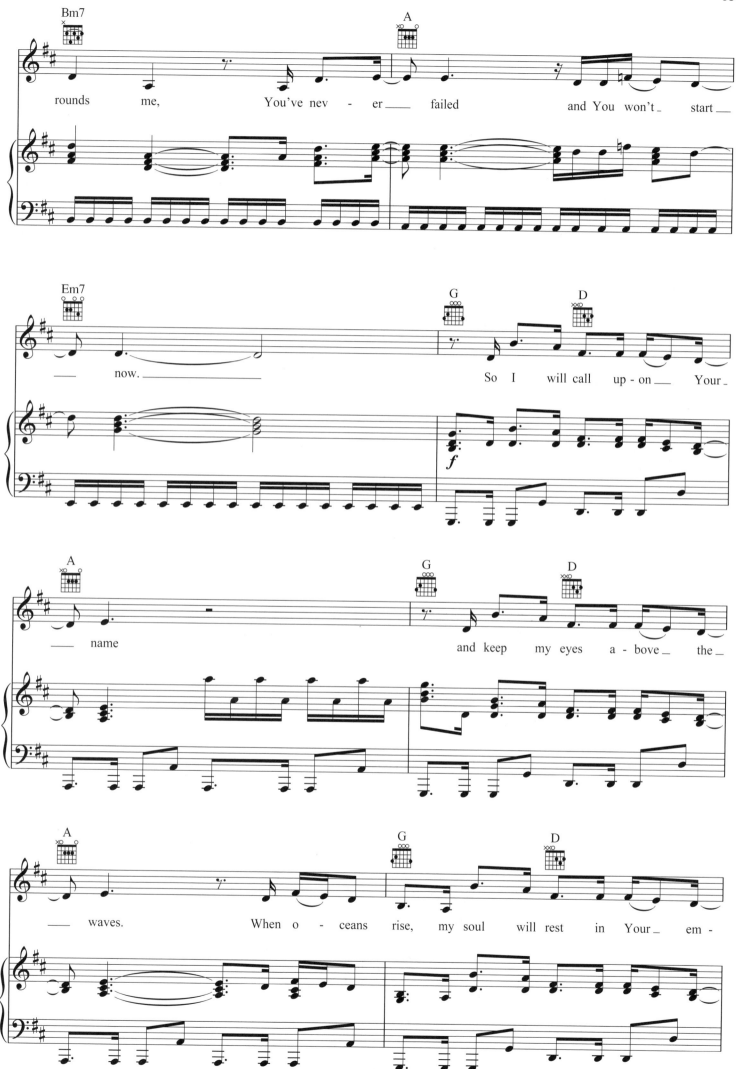

RELENTLESS

Words and Music by JOEL HOUSTON
and MATT CROCKER

With energy

* *Recorded a half step lower.*

THE STAND

Words and Music by
JOEL HOUSTON

With conviction

STRONGER

Words and Music by BEN FIELDING
and REUBEN MORGAN

With praise

Dsus2   A5   Dsus2

A5   D   Esus   A

There is love   that came for us,   hum - bled
ness   none can de - ny,   through the

D   Esus   A   D   E

to   a sin - ner's cross.   You broke my shame   and sin - ful -
storm   and through the fire.   There is truth   that sets me

F#m7   D   E   Dsus2   Esus

ness,   You rose a - gain   vic - to - ri - ous.
free: Je - sus Christ,   who lives in

THIS I BELIEVE
(The Creed)

Words and Music by BEN FIELDING
and MATT CROCKER

Our Fa - ther, ev - er - last - ing,___ the all - cre - at - ing___ One,

God Al - might - y.   Through Your Ho - ly Spir - it,___

___ con - ceiv - ing Christ the___ Son,___ Je - sus our Sav - ior.___

TOUCH THE SKY

Words and Music by JOEL HOUSTON,
DYLAN THOMAS and MICHAEL GUY CHISLETT

What for-tune lies be-yond the __ stars, __ those daz-zling

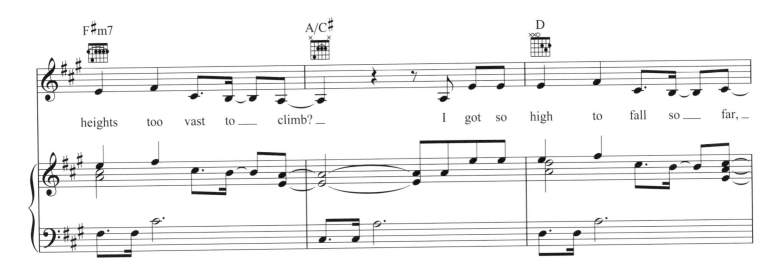

heights too vast to __ climb? __ I got so high to fall so __ far, __

__ but I found heav-en __ as love swept __ low. My heart __ beat-ing, __

Esus
A/C♯
when my knees hit the ground. My heart beat - ing,
f
Dsus2
A/E
F♯m7
my soul breath - ing. I found my life when I laid it down.
A/C♯
Dsus2
A/E
Up - ward fall - ing, spir - it soar - ing. I touch the sky
Esus
A/C♯
when my knees hit the ground. Find me here at Your

WAKE

Words and Music by JOEL DAVIES,
ALEXANDER PAPPAS and HANNAH HOBBS

CONTEMPORARY
Christian Artist Folios

Arranged for Piano, Voice and Guitar

The Jeremy Camp Collection
00307200......................................$17.99

Jeremy Camp – We Cry Out:
The Worship Project
00307178......................................$16.99

Johnny Cash – My Mother's
Hymn Book
00306641......................................$19.99

Casting Crowns – Lifesong
00306748......................................$16.95

Casting Crowns – Come to the
Well
00307346......................................$16.99

Casting Crowns – Until the
Whole World Hears
00307107......................................$16.99

Casting Crowns – The Very
Next Thing
00196585......................................$16.99

The Crabb Family Collection
00233193......................................$16.99

Best of Andrae Crouch –
2nd Edition
00306017......................................$24.99

David Crowder*Band –
Give Us Rest
00307390......................................$16.99

Lauren Daigle – Look Up Child
00284958......................................$19.99

The Kirk Franklin Collection
00307222......................................$24.99

The Greatest Songs of Bill &
Gloria Gaither
00306613......................................$19.99

Keith & Kristyn Getty –
Awaken the Dawn
00123655......................................$11.99

Keith & Kristyn Getty –
In Christ Alone
00123656......................................$11.99

Amy Grant – Greatest Hits
00306948......................................$22.99

Keith Green – The Greatest Hits
00306981......................................$19.99

Keith Green – The Ministry
Years, Volume 1
00306162......................................$29.99

Keith Green –
The Ultimate Collection
00306518......................................$19.99

Steve Green –
The Ultimate Collection
00306784......................................$24.99

Brandon Heath – What If We
00307151......................................$16.99

Israel Houghton – Live from
Another Level
08746591......................................$19.95

Bishop T.D. Jakes & The
Potter's House Mass Choir –
The Storm Is Over
00306456......................................$14.95

Kari Jobe – Where I Find You
00307381......................................$17.99

Days of Elijah – The Best of
Robin Mark
00306944......................................$16.95

The Best of MercyMe - 2nd
Edition
00385971......................................$24.99

MercyMe – Welcome to the New
00128518......................................$16.99

Bart Millard – Hymned No. 1
08746747......................................$15.95

Nicole C. Mullen –
The Ultimate Collection
00307131......................................$17.99

Newsboys – Greatest Hits
00306956......................................$17.95

The Best of Joe Pace
08746468......................................$24.95

Sandi Patti Anthology
00490473......................................$29.99

Elvis Presley -
Songs Of Inspiration
00308175 ....$19.99

Elvis – Ultimate Gospel
00306988......................................$17.99

The Best of Matt Redman
00307080......................................$16.99

Matt Redman –
Sing like Never Before:
The Essential Collection
00116963......................................$19.99

Tenth Avenue North –
Over and Underneath
00307111......................................$16.99

Third Day – Lead Us Back:
Songs of Worship
00145263......................................$16.99

Third Day – Offerings II
All I Have to Give
00306541......................................$16.95

The Best of TobyMac
00113441......................................$24.99

Chris Tomlin –
And If Our God Is for Us
00307187......................................$16.99

Chris Tomlin – Burning Lights
00115644......................................$16.99

The Chris Tomlin Collection –
2nd Edition
00306951......................................$17.99

Chris Tomlin –
How Great Is Our God:
The Essential Collection
00307362......................................$17.99

Chris Tomlin – Love Ran Red
00139166......................................$16.99

Chris Tomlin – Never Lose Sight
00201955......................................$16.99

The Best of Matthew West
00159489......................................$16.99

The Best of Cece Winans
00306912......................................$16.99

Darlene Zschech –
Kiss of Heaven
08739773......................................$16.95

HAL•LEONARD®

7777 W. BLUEMOUND RD. P.O. BOX 13819
MILWAUKEE, WISCONSIN 53213

For a complete listing of the products we have available,
visit us online at www.halleonard.com

The Best
PRAISE & WORSHIP
Songbooks for Piano

Above All
THE PHILLIP KEVEREN SERIES
15 beautiful praise song piano solo arrangements by Phillip Keveren. Includes: Above All • Agnus Dei • Breathe • Draw Me Close • He Is Exalted • I Stand in Awe • Step by Step • We Fall Down • You Are My King (Amazing Love) • and more.
00311024 Piano Solo...................................$12.99

Blended Worship Piano Collection
Songs include: Amazing Grace (My Chains Are Gone) • Be Thou My Vision • Cornerstone • Fairest Lord Jesus • Great Is Thy Faithfulness • How Great Is Our God • I Will Rise • Joyful, Joyful, We Adore Thee • Lamb of God • Majesty • Open the Eyes of My Heart • Praise to the Lord, the Almighty • Shout to the Lord • 10,000 Reasons (Bless the Lord) • Worthy Is the Lamb • Your Name • and more.
00293528 Piano Solo $17.99

Blessings
THE PHILLIP KEVEREN SERIES
Phillip Keveren delivers another stellar collection of piano solo arrangements perfect for any reverent or worship setting: Blessed Be Your Name • Blessings • Cornerstone • Holy Spirit • This Is Amazing Grace • We Believe • Your Great Name • Your Name • and more.
00156601 Piano Solo $12.99

The Best Praise & Worship Songs Ever
80 all-time favorites: Awesome God • Breathe • Days of Elijah • Here I Am to Worship • I Could Sing of Your Love Forever • Open the Eyes of My Heart • Shout to the Lord • We Bow Down • dozens more.
00311057 P/V/G..$22.99

The Big Book of Praise & Worship
Over 50 worship favorites are presented in this popular "Big Book" series collection. Includes: Always • Cornerstone • Forever Reign • I Will Follow • Jesus Paid It All • Lord, I Need You • Mighty to Save • Our God • Stronger • 10,000 Reasons (Bless the Lord) • This Is Amazing Grace • and more.
00140795 P/V/G $24.99

Contemporary Worship Duets
arr. Bill Wolaver
Contains 8 powerful songs carefully arranged by Bill Wolaver as duets for intermediate-level players: Agnus Dei • Be unto Your Name • He Is Exalted • Here I Am to Worship • I Will Rise • The Potter's Hand • Revelation Song • Your Name.
00290593 Piano Duets $10.99

The Best of Passion
Over 40 worship favorites featuring the talents of David Crowder, Matt Redman, Chris Tomlin, and others. Songs include: Always • Awakening • Blessed Be Your Name • Jesus Paid It All • My Heart Is Yours • Our God • 10,000 Reasons (Bless the Lord) • and more.
00101888 P/V/G $19.99

Praise & Worship Duets
THE PHILLIP KEVEREN SERIES
8 worshipful duets by Phillip Keveren: As the Deer • Awesome God • Give Thanks • Great Is the Lord • Lord, I Lift Your Name on High • Shout to the Lord • There Is a Redeemer • We Fall Down.
00311203 Piano Duet $12.99

Shout to the Lord!
THE PHILLIP KEVEREN SERIES
14 favorite praise songs, including: As the Deer • El Shaddai • Give Thanks • Great Is the Lord • How Beautiful • More Precious Than Silver • Oh Lord, You're Beautiful • A Shield About Me • Shine, Jesus, Shine • Shout to the Lord • Thy Word • and more.
00310699 Piano Solo $14.99

Sunday Solos in the Key of C
CLASSIC & CONTEMPORARY WORSHIP SONGS
22 C-major selections, including: Above All • Good Good Father • His Name Is Wonderful • Holy Spirit • Lord, I Need You • Reckless Love • What a Beautiful Name • You Are My All in All • and more.
00301044 Piano Solo $14.99

The Chris Tomlin Collection – 2nd Edition
15 songs from one of the leading artists and composers in Contemporary Christian music, including the favorites: Amazing Grace (My Chains Are Gone) • Holy Is the Lord • How Can I Keep from Singing • How Great Is Our God • Jesus Messiah • Our God • We Fall Down • and more.
00306951 P/V/G $17.99

Top Christian Downloads
21 of Christian music's top hits are presented in this collection of intermediate level piano solo arrangements. Includes: Forever Reign • How Great Is Our God • Mighty to Save • Praise You in This Storm • 10,000 Reasons (Bless the Lord) • Your Grace Is Enough • and more.
00125051 Piano Solo................................$14.99

Top 25 Worship Songs
25 contemporary worship hits includes: Glorious Day (Passion) • Good, Good Father (Chris Tomlin) • Holy Spirit (Francesca Battistelli) • King of My Heart (John Mark & Sarah McMillan) • The Lion and the Lamb (Big Daddy Weave) • Reckless Love (Cory Asbury) • 10,000 Reasons (Matt Redman) • This Is Amazing Grace (Phil Wickham) • What a Beautiful Name (Hillsong Worship) • and more.
00288610 P/V/G $17.99

Top Worship Downloads
20 of today's chart-topping Christian hits, including: Cornerstone • Forever Reign • Great I Am • Here for You • Lord, I Need You • My God • Never Once • One Thing Remains (Your Love Never Fails) • Your Great Name • and more.
00120870 P/V/G $16.99

The World's Greatest Praise Songs
Shawnee Press
This is a unique and useful collection of 50 of the very best praise titles of the last three decades. Includes: Above All • Forever • Here I Am to Worship • I Could Sing of Your Love Forever • Open the Eyes of My Heart • and so many more.
35022891 P/V/G $19.99

HAL•LEONARD®
www.halleonard.com
P/V/G = Piano/Vocal/Guitar Arrangements